# EXTRATRANSMISSION

# EXTRATRANSMISSION

ANDREA ABI-KARAM

KELSEY STREET PRESS

*FIRSTS!*

KELSEY STREET PRESS

2824 Kelsey Street, Berkeley, CA 94705

info@kelseyst.com  www.kelseyst.com

Library of Congress Cataloging-in-Publication Data

Names: Abi-Karam, Andrea, 1989– author.

Title: EXTRATRANSMISSION / Andrea Abi-Karam.

Description: Berkeley, CA : Kelsey Street Press, [2019]

Identifiers: LCCN 2018041745 | ISBN 9780932716897 (pbk. : alk. paper)

Classification: LCC PS3601.B5 E97 2018 | DDC 818/.607—dc23

LC record available at https://lccn.loc.gov/2018041745

Designed by Quemadura

Illustration on cover and p. ii by Andrea Abi-Karam

Typefaces designed by Sibylle Hagmann and Zuzana Licko

Edited by Mg Roberts

Printed on acid-free, recycled paper

in the United States of America

# Contents

# EXTRATRANSMISSION

# KILL BRO / KILL COP

I USED TO WORK IN A LAB WITH RATS FOR A LONG TIME. A
MEMORY LAB. WE WERE TRYING TO FIGURE OUT WHAT PART
OF THEIR TINY BRAINS COULD REMEMBER HOW TO NAVIGATE
SPACE. WHAT TOLD THEM WHICH WAY TO GO.


A MODEL FOR HUMANS

A MODEL FOR 'CURING ALZHEIMER'S'

A MODEL FOR NAVIGATION

A MODEL FOR HUMANLESS NAVIGATION

.


A MODEL FOR DRONES

I QUIT SHORTLY AFTER THE LAB GOT FUNDING FROM THE
US            DEPARTMENT            OF            DEFENSE.

DID U KNOW THAT IF YR A COMBAT VETERAN WITH PTSD U CAN GET A NONPROFIT THAT IS FUNDED BY THE CIA TO GIVE U A DOG?

I WANT A DOG.

CHECK 1—check, check

CHECK 2—check?

CHECK 3—can you hear me?

CHECK 4—is the room empty?

CHECK 5—can you hear me?

CHECK 6—oh well.

CHECK 7—my story is empty, anyway

CHECK 8—lights off.

CHECK 9—goodnight.

CHECK 10—NEXT ON CNN: a poetry of directness:
kill all the noise bros who move to Brooklyn & tell everyone
desperately that the noise they're making is the only thing they
believe in. kill all the bro poets. actually you know what, kill all the
bros. kill all the power dynamics in the room. kill all the power
dynamics in the white room. kill all the power dynamics in all the
rooms. pull them down by their greasy cables. get yr hands dirty.
kill all the hierarchies of power of who is publishing who & who
is fucking who & who they fucked before they got published.
publish who they fucked, or don't. kill the nonprofit board of poets
who scheduled the endless summer reading during dyke march this
saturday. & kill the sociality that makes queers feel excluded & that
makes the orgy dangerous for our bodies & that makes you select

who to make eye contact with & who to ignore on alternating nights & which beer to schedule on which day & which bar to go to after which reading. & kill the system that was designed to alienate everyone from each other & that caused this desperate sociality to emerge & kill the system of gendered power that makes it so hard to inhabit every moment in my own skin to know how to detect each buzz like counting the number of trains that pass at night. & kill the language of avoidance that made it so hard for me to write this. CHECK 11—is anybody out there?

on the surface of the signature injury

on the surface

CIRCLE ONE OPTION BELOW:

MILD

MODERATE

SEVERE

in the framework of it all the female body in combat reads
differently                    computes                    differently
glitches    differently    that    the    female    body    in
combat is not a state of on opposed to off. it's a state of always on.
always watching. waiting for the moment of the signature injury—
whatever it might be. it costs so much to maintain the body in con-
stant combat. it must consume & consume & consume just to stay
awake. before it burns it all away too fast. she gnaws at her own fin-
gertips to stay alert, to stay awake, to stay warm. easy to get cold out
there in the desert at night. hard to maintain the skin sealed to the
bones below, to the meat beneath against each blast & every impact.
the environment tries to pull it apart—make little entrances for it-
self—ports to communicate information back to the base, shuttle
information back up the chain of command. ports to communicate
information ports to channel energy into the surroundings—static
shoots across the dry desert air. as if it's not enough to just exist in
constant combat command wants the full download the full extra-
transmission she's tried so hard to keep sewn strictly in. direct line
to read each electric impulse each time a muscle moves. brace.
unbrace. skin just a shell plastick sheeting to keep the muscle moist.
a case for your new iphone X. release innermost secrets through your
fingertips. eyes just a mirror, a high resolution scan of the surround-
ings. breaks in vision noted. breaks in brush noted.

lack of cover. noted. body just a case for desirable information until they get a new shipment in of those who must volunteer their own skin cases to protect the TV set stationed in your living room. to enter combat. to take orders. to take the fall. every body is consumable. every american body is consumable. there's a whole country back home to manufacture more willing bodies for the volunteer based army. a country that sometimes agrees to relax its borders in exchange for the combat ready body. for the soft skin that caves in from every bit of shrapnel. for the soft skull that splits on impact. for the soft brain that bounces back and forth inside the skull. for the soft brain that tears & swells. for the soft brain that after the tears & swells still turns the body back on. still serves. for the soft person who can't remember.

on the assembly line to american nationalism

little clicks along the conveyor belt

*As of 2017 375,230 US troops have sustained a traumatic brain injury (TBI).*

*TBIs are the signature injury of the war on terror. they are severe concussions where past memories are erased and daily memory continues to be difficult. yr in an armored vehicle somewhere in iraq or afghanistan. on a desert road. not a lot of cover. and yr vehicle gets hit by a rocket propelled grenade or you drive over the tripwire for an improvised explosive device.*

*there is a blast. you are thrown into the wall or the roof or the ground. yr body hits the wall or the roof or the ground hard. with force. bones break. yr brain moves forward and back against the inside of yr skull like all those really sick drunk driving movies where no one survives that you have to watch in driver's ed when yr 16. it's like that. except you survive. the blast, get up & run. yr body survives but you now have to cope with becoming a new person.*

THIS SONG IS ABOUT ABUSIVE RELATIONSHIPS

I TOLD EVERYONE ALL OVER THE COUNTRY.

FROM LA TO KANSAS CITY TO MINNEAPOLIS.


MAYBE U LISTENED, MAYBE U DIDN'T

                                        turn me up NOW


                    DID U THINK IT WOULD COME TO

                    THIS

                    I WILL EXTRACT U FROM BENEATH MY

                    SKIN

                    SHORT OUT THE WIRES UNTIL THE

                    END


THIS IS THE END OF MY SKIN

MAYBE WHAT I ACTUALLY WANT IS TO NOT SEE THE PLANTS
MARKED DROUGHT RESISTANT AT HOME DEPOT & I DEFINITELY
WANT TO STOP CARING ABOUT THE AUDIENCE BUT I STILL
WANT U 2 CARE ABOUT ME


FAKE IT TIL U MAKE IT

FAKE IT TIL U MARKET

FAKE IT TIL U MARK. IT.

TO THE PUNK BRO WHO TOLD ME I HAD BRUTAL EYEBALLS:

U R SUCH A WHINER. U FOLLOWED ME OUT OF THE PIT & SAID
I LOOKED AT U IN THE EYES B4 I PUNCHED U DIRECTLY IN THE
STOMACH. IT WAS 100 DEGREES & DARK. IT COULD HAVE BEEN
ANYONE. YR DUMB ROOMMATE OR YR DUMB FRIEND. U STEPPED
CLOSER TO TELL ME I HAD BRUTAL EYEBALLS. OVER & OVER &
SO THIS TIME I PUNCHED U IN THE STOMACH WITH MY HALF
EMPTY 40OZ DIGGING THE CAP IN DEEP THRU TO YR KIDNEYS.
LEAVING HIGHLIFE CAP RIDGES ON YR STUPID SHIRTLESS CAVED
IN STOMACH UNTIL U PUKED ON YR OWN SHOES.

I HOPE YR GF LIKES THE BRUISES.

TO THE COP WHO READ MY TEXT MESSAGES:

I STILL REMEMBER YR FACE. WHITE AND PINK AND SOFT W GREY HAIR. U COULD BE MY POETRY PROFESSOR, MY SUGAR DADDY IF U HELD ANOTHER SYMBOL OF POWER BETWEEN YR THICK HANDS KNUCKLES THROBBING ADRENALIN PUMPING WITH THE EXCITEMENT OF FINALLY CATCHING ME. IF U HELD A BOOK OR YR COCK INSTEAD OF A BATON CUMMING AFTER ME. I LUST AFTER THE MOMENT I CAN BECOME INVISIBLE AND PLUNGE A SCREWDRIVER INTO YR EYEBALL THE ONE ON THE LEFT THAT GLIMPSED ME FROM AROUND THE CORNER OF THE BUILDING WHOSE SHADE I SPRINTED UNDER A SCREWDRIVER WITH A FLAT HEAD TO SCRAPE AGAINST THE INSIDE OF YR SKULL WHILE YR LEFT EYE WATCHES FROM A CRACK IN THE SIDEWALK.

I HAVE TOOLS TOO.

TO THE BRO POET @ MY READING LOOKING @ HIS IPHONE:

CAN'T WAIT TO SHOVE THAT IPHONE BETWEEN YR 6TH & 7TH
RIBS. LET'S SEE HOW IMPORTANT YR FAKE FRIEND'S STATUS
UPDATE IS FROM INSIDE YR LEFT LUNG. & FOR THE LOVE OF
GOD STOP WRITING NOW THAT U CAN'T TALK. OR BREATHE.

TO THE NOISE BRO WHO COCKBLOCKED ME:

THERE U WERE SWAYING YR HEAD TO UNINTELLIGIBLE NOISE
THAT U PROB FELT WAS THE MOST IMPORTANT UNINTELLIGI-
BLE NOISE EVER. THAT EVERY1 MUST LISTEN. IT GAVE ME A
FUCKIN HEADACHE. HOW U TRAILED HER AFTER THE SHOW
EVEN THO U WERE NOT INVITED. I MEAN I WAS ONLY IN TOWN
FOR ONE NIGHT, ONE TIME A YEAR CAN U JUST. NOT. WHEN I
RETURN I'LL BE SURE TO GRAB YR HAIR AND DRIVE A BALL.
POINT. PEN. THROUGH YR EARS. OUTER EAR CANAL. INNER
EAR CANAL. EAR DRUM. PIERCED & BLOWN OUT. I'LL DO IT
HARD DON'T WORRY. I'LL DO IT HARD SO THE BLACK INK
DRIBBLES OUT OF YR EARS LIKE IT DOES OUT OF JOHNNY
DEPP'S EYES IN THAT MOVIE AS I LEAVE U ON THE STICKY
FLOOR OF SOME OTHER STUPID SHOW I LEAVE U NOW WITH
THICK WET SILENCE AGAINST ALL THE
SHITTY NOISE YR FRIENDS MAKE.


U SHD THANK ME.

he wore shirts with bands i liked on them. he wore 100$ levis that he ripped open on purpose until i ripped them all off and stole his wallet. it was raining. it never rains.

WHY DID U STAND ME UP LAST NIGHT. I WAS THERE WAITING 4 U IN THE DARK BOOTS DOUBLE KNOTTED, ANKLES BRACED FOR THE MOMENT WHEN THE BASS WAS DIRTY AND THE BLAST BEATS SHOOK THE FLOOR TO DRIVE MY ELBOW INTO YR GUT FOR EVEN DARING TO RUN INTO ME. IT WOULD HAVE BEEN FUN. MAKE SURE U SHOW NEXT TIME.

TO THE SPORTS BRO WHO ASKED IF I WAS MARRIED, GIRL:

SEND 1000$ TO P.O. BOX #3825968 FOR YR STUPIDITY IN MY PRESENCE. IF U FAIL TO DO THIS I'LL BE WAITING 4 U @ THE NEXT GAME, CHAINRING IN HAND READY TO PIERCE 44 HOLES INTO THE SIDE OF YR NECK PRESSING EACH TOOTH IN ONE. BY. ONE. I CAN'T WAIT 2 WATCH THE RED OF YR PRECIOUS 9NERS STREAM DOWN & MIX W THE GOLD OF YR STUPID JERSEY WHILE U COLLAPSE & PASS OUT 4VR.

I KNOW U'LL BE 2 WASTED TO DODGE ME.

TO THE TECH BRO WHO NEVER TIPS:

NEXT TIME U COME IN HERE FOR A "NETWORKING" MEETING & ORDER A TRIPLE EXTRA HOT MOCHA & PAY W YR BLACK "SPE-CIAL" AMEX CARD LEAVING THE TIP LINE EMPTY YR EXTRA HOT BS DRINK IS GOING IN YR FACE RIGHT AT THE THIN LIPS U USE TO "NETWORK" W & YR METAL BLACK AMEX THAT ALWAYS GLITCHES OUR REGISTER I WILL USE AS A KNIFE TO SLICE OFF THE FINGERS U USE TO WRITE EMAILS W. WHILE U RUN & SCREAM OUT OF MY CAFE I'LL SLIP THE BLOODY CREDIT CARD IN MY BACK POCKET. THX 4 PAYING OFF MY STUDENT LOANS BRO.

TO THE NEXT TECH BRO WHO COMES IN HERE:

YR GETTING SEVERED FINGERS

INSTEAD OF FRIES.

FRY THEM UP.

YUM.

KILL THE BRO IN YR HEAD

TO MYSELF:

PULL EACH SINEWY THREAD OUT ONE BY ONE TRACING THEM
ACROSS YR TONGUE. THEY ARE SHARP & AFTER A MOMENT OF
GLORIOUS TASTE THERE IS COPPER THAT OVERRIDES IT. THE
STRANDS SLICE. FOR EVERY FEMALE BODY U HAVE THOUGHT OF
IN OBSESSIVE WAYS. THE SLICES FORM STAR PATTERNS ON YR
TONGUE. THEY STING & STRETCH WHEN U TRY TO SPEAK. I COULD
BE ANY OF U SITTING THERE. READING. REMEMBER THAT.

# DECREATION

select a PDA from the moving belt.

slide the PDA all the way in to the port.

it should not hurt.

it should feel comfortable.

it should feel natural.

there may be initial misfirings.

you may see scans of the calendar behind the eyes. they will feel like dreams.


you won't miss any appointments.

& remember, it's just a prototype,

you will not be satisfied.

HEAD ON COLLISION


DOUBLE VISION

THIS IS NOT I FORGOT MY WALLET AT HOME DURING MERCURY
RETROGRADE

THIS IS NOT OH I FORGOT U 2 EVEN DATED SRY IF IT'S AWK
NOW THAT WE'RE FUCKING

THIS IS NOT I DON'T REMEMBER SPRAINING MY ANKLE BC I
WAS WASTED BUT NOW IT HURTS SOMETIMES

THIS IS NOT TEXTBOOK PTSD

THIS IS THE END OF THE CANON & AN ATTEMPT TO ADAPT IN A
WORLD THAT CONSTANTLY FAILS ME

THIS IS THE END OF A PERSON & THE BEGINNING OF A
MALF(X)ING CYBORG

AN IRREVERSIBLE DETACHMENT FROM MY BODY

A WALKING GHOST.

THIS IS ABOUT HOW THE AMERICAN TRAGEDY ISN'T ABOUT ALL THE WALKING GHOSTS.

HOW THE AMERICAN TRAGEDY IS THAT SOME FEMALE COMBAT-ANTS CAN'T REMEMBER GIVING BIRTH OR BEING MARRIED. IT'S ABOUT PRODUCTION & REPRODUCTION MOTHERS MAKE MORE MALLEABLE SOFT SKIN. MARRIAGE MAKES MORE ESCALATING ISOLATION. GHOSTS AREN'T PRODUCTIVE BUT SOMETIMES NON-PROFITS HELP THEM GET JOBS.

AT WHAT POINT DID U REALIZE THERE WAS

SOMETHING VERY VERY WRONG?

## SIGNATURE SYMPTOMS OF THE TRAUMATIC BRAIN

I     N     J     U     R     Y

i can recall almost nothing from the before. i trip up the stairs regu-
larly. my body fails me over & over. i can't stand having to pay atten-
tion. i can't stand not understanding. i can't can't find my words or
even speak them without pausing. the therapist says i'm depressed &
that loud sounds set me off because i have PTSD. i don't know myself
or my body or my so called family. the only time i feel like i can stand
on my own is during therapeutic animal therapy

re route the connections until they are no longer tense until they are 'at rest' until the hips forget what it means to clench when hitting the sidewalk. i want to hold my eyeballs in my hands. wrap them up so no light gets through. that's the best way for what comes next. take a pair of TRAUMA shears and slip the fingers from yr dominant hand through the loops of the handle. now it's time to turn it off and get cut off from the WORLD WIDE VIEW yr connected to. cut the wires emerging from the back of the eyeball one by one—to lessen the shock (NOTE: be careful not to cut the meaty ones or you will actually be blind, just cut the latex encased ones / they feel like wet plastick) (NOTE2: if yr having difficulty guiding yr hands through this process, do it one eyeball at a time and position the resting eyeball at a 90 degree angle to the eyeball getting work done to help yr hands navigate from shear to wire. DO THE CUTTING CAREFULLY, as the wires have been sitting inside yr body yr entire life and are very slippery. don't let the fiber optic wires fool you—you'll know you've done the job right when you suddenly feel the crushing alienation of being cut off from THE NET-WORK, when you no longer feel INTEGRATED. yr different parts feel at risk of coming apart from the whole. it will be uncomfortable.

WHAT U CAN'T SEE CAN'T HURT U

it's just a story. some story someone else told me. some story about why i have stretch marks. some story about why the kid cries at 2am every night. some story about how i'm supposed to care. some story that says i'm lucky to be alive, i should be grateful. i don't really feel alive. ghost in my own skin. it's like people have a relationship to my face but not what's behind it, my ghost-self, the one i left in the desert, the part i can't ever tap into. i look at pictures every night, pictures of me, pictures of people i don't recognize. you tell me the names that belong to the faces. i repeat them. you ask if i remember them. i say yes just for you.

DO U REMEMBER THE BLAST?

there are stories of machines. stories of machines that enter bodies machines that enter armor. pierce. the. skin. machines that force their way through. machines that force. machines that force their way through boundaries, through borders, through armored shells, through skin. just a few scratches & bruises. bump on the head. nothing major. right major. yes major. right, left major. keep moving keep driving keep fighting. worry about the bruises later.

THERE IS A BLAST

THERE IS AN IMPACT

THERE IS THE WALL OR THE ROOF OR THE GROUND

THERE IS A BLAST AN IMPACT A FORCE AGAINST U

THERE IS THE WALL THE ROOF THE GROUND THE SHARP

METAL EDGE

THERE IS A BLAST

AND THAT'S IT

# FUSION

SIGNATURE SYMPTOMS OF MY WORLD


—GOING DEAF IN ONE EAR

—UNWANTED MEMORIES

—BLEEDING UNDER THE FINGERNAILS

—INABILITY TO BE PRESENT

—$$$ THERAPY BILLS

—EMOTIONAL EXHAUSTION

—BELIEF IN OTHER NIGHTMARES, IN OTHER WAYS 2

S       U       R       V       I       V       E

i pull wires out of my skin just below the surface of the screen. i tap on them to make them activate—thicken—awaken. i tap on them at the inside of the elbow—thick—material. i take a new razor blade out of the package from the hardware store and make an incision on my forearm close to the inside of my elbow. i massage it open. i pull the wire out slowly—do not to pull anything else out at this time. the wire is wet from being inside my body. it won't short out—these wires were built for my body. i drop the wire into a clear plastick bucket at my feet where it rejoins the wires it used to connect with inside my body. communication exoskeleton.

ports on the inside of my wrist that fail to connect that fail to remember for me i'm waiting to connect i need to connect without this connection i am alone i desire control of the connection from the inside of my wrist to my brain. what gets sent. what gets translated. i pick at the thinner wires that reach out of the tops of my arms. pull them out quickly, a little resistance and then the skin lets go.

sometimes the ports on the inside of the wrist throb & ooze. like all the blood rushes to the point of fusion on the inside of the wrist. the blood rushes & the skin swells around it—will it be rejected? the port rises at an angle making it difficult to plug in quickly, tap in easily, flick on smoothly. i'd heard of there being complications with this kind of body mod—but i never thought it would happen to me. that i would glitch the way they expected. i'm supposed to glitch differently—encounter pulses differently—encounter my self differently. i feel it sometimes, am aware of it, dragging against the inside of my shirtsleeves, the outside of my jeans. hope it doesn't snag on the little metal teeth i use to read the world outside myself.

how to become a new glitch, a new disruption?

grow      a      new      port—a      new      port      of
internal      to      external      connection.      a      new      point      of
f      u      s      i      o      n
not      as      a      systematized      control      of      the
pulse—signal—buzz—datapkg—but      as      a      point      of      disruption.

# EXTRA
# TRANS
# MISSION

I CAN YELL AT U ALL I WANT BUT STILL NOBODY ELSE KNOWS
WHAT'S GOING ON

I JUST NEED TO FIND MY WORDS

TEACH ME HOW TO

REMEMBER. HOW TO BECOME

A          NEW          PERSON.

TEACH ME HOW NOT TO GET LOST IN

THE MAZE. TEACH ME HOW TO BECOME

A          NEW          RAT.

I'M NOT TRYING TO REMEMBER FOR U OR FORGET W U. I'M
JUST TRYING TO UNDERSTAND HOW IT ALL WORKS. U HAVE THE
PDA TO REMEMBER FOR U. OR MAYBE IT'S AN IPHONE OR A TAB-
LET. I LIKE SAYING PDA THO—IT'S MORE GENERAL. NOT ABOUT
THE MAKE BUT THE FUNCTION. YR EXTERNAL BRAIN. HOLDING
YR BRAIN IN THE PALM OF YR HAND SLEEK AND SLIM. NOT WET
LIKE THE OTHER STUFF WE'VE PULLED OUT. HOLDING YR BRAIN
IN THE PALM OF YR HAND. I WONDER HOW IT FEELS WHEN U
TURN IT OFF. IT MUST BE NICE TO TURN IT OFF.

there is no pleasure in this language. in this flatness. in this practical prosthesis. my palm is just a function. liquid crystal regulation. right major. left major. worry about the cracks later. turn it off now & slide it out.

i look out beyond the glass pasted on my face
& i can't see anything that i want.
i'm already disconnected—eyes no longer the lens of the
WORLD WIDE VIEW
just for me—
one      malf(x)ing      cyborg      among      many

it feels important
to remember the before—

                                                                    not everyone can




of course i know that—
sometimes i can but don't want to
& sometimes you just can't




                                                                    i just can't




& sometimes i can & have to
not forget the source
not forget the shitty relationship
or the shitty cop or all the damn bros.
where there was skin before machine
& machine before skin

i wonder if it's really up there
all of our memories above us
in the electrostatic cloud


i look up sometimes just to try & see it
try & catch a glimpse
of purple lightning shooting across


from point to point
moment to moment


MEMORY


TO MEMORY

but you can't hit the download button
& have them dropped into the ball
of wires in yr hand, wait for them to
travel back into yr body

BACK    INTO    THE    PLACES    THEY    USED    TO    LIVE

i know that. don't you
think i know that
it's too damn late
that i lost the download code
in the desert

THE STATE GAVE U THE PDA BUT IT ALSO GAVE U THE INJURY


WHICH CAME FIRST


THE INJURY OR THE TECH?


                                        THE INJURY
                                IT'S ALWAYS THE INJURY

WHAT IF I NEED THIS HAND FOR SOMETHING ELSE. TO STAB
THE COP IN THE EYE WITH THE SCREWDRIVER OR THE BRO IN
THE EAR WITH THE PEN.

OR TO GET ME OFF. INSTEAD OF

GETTING ME THERE ON TIME.

IT'S JUST NOT COMING TOGETHER

IT'S JUST

NOT

ON THE OUTSIDE LOOKING IN

IT WAS JUST A LITTLE BIT DANGEROUS

IT DOESN'T SEEM LIKE ANYTHING IS WRONG.

BUT SO MUCH IS. SO SO MUCH.

U TOLD ME THAT ALREADY

I KNOW

I KNOW IT'S NOT JUST GOING TO GO AWAY. THAT'S WHY

THIS FEELS SO NECESSARY

ON THE OUTSIDE LOOKING IN

IS THIS WHAT U SIGNED UP FOR

IS THIS WHAT U SIGNED UP FOR

IS THIS WHAT U SIGNED UP FOR

IS THIS WHAT U SIGNED UP FOR

IS THIS WHAT U SIGNED UP FOR

IS THIS WHAT U SIGNED UP FOR

IS THIS WHAT U SIGNED UP FOR

IS THIS WHAT U SIGNED UP FOR

IS THIS WHAT U SIGNED UP FOR

IS THIS WHAT U SIGNED UP FOR

IS THIS WHAT U SIGNED UP FOR

IS THIS WHAT U SIGNED UP FOR

IS THIS WHAT U SIGNED UP FOR

IS THIS WHAT U SIGNED UP FOR

IS THIS WHAT U SIGNED UP FOR

IS THIS WHAT U SIGNED UP FOR

IS THIS WHAT U SIGNED UP FOR

IS THIS WHAT U SIGNED UP FOR

IS THIS WHAT U SIGNED UP FOR

IS THIS WHAT U SIGNED UP FOR

IS THIS WHAT U SIGNED UP FOR

IS THIS WHAT U SIGNED UP FOR

IS THIS WHAT U SIGNED UP FOR

IS THIS WHAT U SIGNED UP FOR

IS THIS WHAT U SIGNED UP FOR

IS THIS WHAT U SIGNED UP FOR

IS THIS WHAT U SIGNED UP FOR

IS THIS WHAT U SIGNED UP FOR

IS THIS WHAT U SIGNED UP FOR

IS THIS WHAT U SIGNED UP FOR

IS THIS WHAT U SIGNED UP FOR

IS THIS WHAT U SIGNED UP FOR

IS THIS WHAT U SIGNED UP FOR

IS THIS WHAT U SIGNED UP FOR

IS THIS WHAT U SIGNED UP FOR

IS THIS WHAT U SIGNED UP FOR

IS THIS WHAT U SIGNED UP FOR
IS THIS WHAT U SIGNED UP FOR
IS THIS WHAT U SIGNED UP FOR
IS THIS WHAT U SIGNED UP FOR
IS THIS WHAT U SIGNED UP FOR
IS THIS WHAT U SIGNED UP FOR
IS THIS WHAT U SIGNED UP FOR
IS THIS WHAT U SIGNED UP FOR
IS THIS WHAT U SIGNED UP FOR
IS THIS WHAT U SIGNED UP FOR
IS THIS WHAT U SIGNED UP FOR
IS THIS WHAT U SIGNED UP FOR
IS THIS WHAT U SIGNED UP FOR
IS THIS WHAT U SIGNED UP FOR
IS THIS WHAT U SIGNED UP FOR
IS THIS WHAT U SIGNED UP FOR
IS THIS WHAT U SIGNED UP FOR
IS THIS WHAT U SIGNED UP FOR
IS THIS WHAT U SIGNED UP FOR
IS THIS WHAT U SIGNED UP FOR
IS THIS WHAT U SIGNED UP FOR
IS THIS WHAT U SIGNED UP FOR
IS THIS WHAT U SIGNED UP FOR
IS THIS WHAT U SIGNED UP FOR
IS THIS WHAT U SIGNED UP FOR
IS THIS WHAT U SIGNED UP FOR
IS THIS WHAT U SIGNED UP FOR
IS THIS WHAT U SIGNED UP FOR
IS THIS WHAT U SIGNED UP FOR
IS THIS WHAT U SIGNED UP FOR
IS THIS WHAT U SIGNED UP FOR
IS THIS WHAT U SIGNED UP FOR
IS THIS WHAT U SIGNED UP FOR
IS THIS WHAT U SIGNED UP FOR
IS THIS WHAT U SIGNED UP FOR

A GHOST THAT WOULD LIVE ON & ON

I AM

CHOOSING ELEMENTS FROM A SOURCE DOCUMENT

I AM

OBSESSING OVER SO MANY THINGS

I AM

TRYING TO THINK ABOUT BODY AUTONOMY

I AM

TRYING TO GET OFF

I AM

TRYING TO SHORT OUT

THERE IS A BLAST

THERE IS AN IMPACT

THERE IS THE INFORMATION THE ELECTRICITY THE

SHRAPNEL THE BODIES THE FEELING

THERE IS THE SHARP METAL EDGE

THERE IS A BLAST

AND

EMOTIONAL OR PHYSICAL WOUNDS U CAN RIDE
THERAPEUTIC HORSES FOR FREE?

DID U KNOW THAT IF YR A COMBAT VETERAN WITH
EMOTIONAL OR PHYSICAL WOUNDS U CAN RIDE
THERAPEUTIC HORSES FOR FREE?

DID U KNOW THAT IF YR A COMBAT VETERAN WITH
EMOTIONAL OR PHYSICAL WOUNDS U CAN RIDE
THERAPEUTIC HORSES FOR FREE?

DID U KNOW THAT IF YR A COMBAT VETERAN WITH
EMOTIONAL OR PHYSICAL WOUNDS U CAN RIDE
THERAPEUTIC HORSES FOR FREE?

DID U KNOW THAT IF YR A COMBAT VETERAN WITH
EMOTIONAL OR PHYSICAL WOUNDS U CAN RIDE
THERAPEUTIC HORSES FOR FREE?

DID U KNOW THAT IF YR A COMBAT VETERAN WITH
EMOTIONAL OR PHYSICAL WOUNDS U CAN RIDE
THERAPEUTIC HORSES FOR FREE?

DID U KNOW THAT IF YR A COMBAT VETERAN WITH
EMOTIONAL OR PHYSICAL WOUNDS U CAN RIDE
THERAPEUTIC HORSES FOR FREE?

DID U KNOW THAT IF YR A COMBAT VETERAN WITH
EMOTIONAL OR PHYSICAL WOUNDS U CAN RIDE
THERAPEUTIC HORSES FOR FREE?

DID U KNOW THAT IF YR A COMBAT VETERAN WITH
EMOTIONAL OR PHYSICAL WOUNDS U CAN RIDE
THERAPEUTIC HORSES FOR FREE?

DID U KNOW THAT IF YR A COMBAT VETERAN WITH
EMOTIONAL OR PHYSICAL WOUNDS U CAN RIDE
THERAPEUTIC HORSES FOR FREE?

standing—knees locked

so i don't collapse even if
i doze off

i wait for yr touch.

like i know how hard it is
to feel alone—when i'm alone
in the stable too long
i start to chew on wood
just like you did the feet
of your grandmother's rocking chair
when you needed more
care like you needed after the blast
how you need someone to take
care of you instead of you
trying to take care of the whole
country

until suddenly everyone around you
noticed you were struggling
to find yr words to find yr names to find yr memories
—but first they dropped yr rank—
failing to follow orders, how could you
such a grave offense in a nation
held up by a steel ladder
manufactured in china


obey—or get pushed to the edges
it's more vulnerable there but
at least you can see the outside
of that moment they failed you.
this failure makes it difficult to trust them.
if i have a trainer who wavers, even for a moment
i don't trust he'll be there for me

i need to keep him sharp

next time he tries to ruffle my mane
i'll rear. i'll box the air to remind him

i could crush his panicked head
beneath my heels

he won't pet me for a week after.

he remembers the precarity of his life
in this way he can't control
in this way you couldn't possibly
control the blast—he remembers
looking up at the bottoms of my
hooves & i remember his inconsistencies
you remember waking up & i remember
the first time you came to see me
you pet me like you had never
needed your palms to be against
something more than my body
and i rocked in
remembering each night i'd spent
coughing up splinters

when you touch my hair
in morning light
to wake me from standing sleep
to go & walk together
even if it's in a circle
over & over
the same grind
that we can be there
& feel the static
my mane tangled between your fingers
bristles between the teeth of yr port

or how you always have to go
& i have to stay—what if one day
you could take me with you
beyond the gate
beyond this one type of experience
we always share together

tell me—do you sleep standing too?

out there in the desert seeking safety
beneath endless explosions with no cover

i don't think i would make it out there.

i don't think i would make it out there
like you did or that part of you that did—
my instinct is to run to just run fast & far—
i know i wouldn't make it that way either
that i would trample across a tripwire
hooves heavy with exhaustion
that would be my total end
& hopefully i wouldn't have to remember
that it'd be over fast. sometimes i
don't know what's worse for you the fact
that you can't remember or do you not want to?
i think that you remember meeting me
week after week, or at least
i hope that you do

people think horses scare easily
always haunted by the way we sleep
standing, always ready to escape if
we have to

that we are haunted by the possibility of the future

& you are haunted by the possibility of what lives in the past—
yr own self
trapped standing alone in the desert

the fawn understands this dissonance because the fawn wandered from a natural place to an unnatural place. or maybe it didn't. i am not sure that it matters. but the fawn is running on the streets & its hooves are bleeding from slapping the concrete day after day, night after night & the fawn begins to slow down. there are obstacles. big metal monsters with red or white eyes that move much faster than the fawn. it has to stay out of the way in order to survive. the fawn is tired & slips through a break in a fence into an empty building. there are piles of rubble. the inside doesn't look like anything yet but there is a feeling that it used to be something. the fawn climbs to a higher level up these slippery concrete stairs to get out of the awful orange work lights that hang from pillars on the first level. there are small windows on every floor but the view of the city lights is muted through shiny white sheets of plastick. the building is wrapped in this plastick maybe to keep out water throughout the remodel maybe it's so no one but the fawn can sneak in. maybe it's for obscurity, so no one knows what's going on even though you can probably just find out on the internet that uber is moving in. that there is no hope. that downtown is totally fucked. but the building is wrapped in plastick which is a surface with tension & slick texture. a surface that can be written on & also punctured. the building is in a moment of transition. the plastick protects, at least conceptually, the transition to continue as long as it is wrapped. they're probably carving windows into the exterior. big windows for CEOs to look out of & down onto the little people on the street. big windows that probably aren't earthquake resistant. big windows for small bodies. the fawn finds a scrap of plastick on an upper level & lays down on it to avoid the cold of the musty cement floor. the fawn's hooves are cracked & dry from clicking across the pavement in order

to find

something still.

there's something still about an empty building, something that is frozen, still nothing even though it could be so many things. a location for generator shows, squat space, a place before it becomes something slick & clean—a place before it is something. tonight it is a place for the fawn to sleep. i lay down next to the fawn who shares the scrap of plastick with me. for me it is a contested space a place where people have gathered as it dissolves, the windows being carved out from the frame, old signs being taken down, the roof being made safe to eat lunch on between business meetings. i listen to the fawn's breath slow & wonder if the fawn will stay here tomorrow too & the next night & the next night. i know that the workers will find the fawn eventually & the fawn will have to leave. this i know—that the fawn cannot stay—that i cannot stay no matter how much i would love to throw a party or a show or a reading on one of the dusty upper levels of the old sears building. but i know they will find me too. the fawn's hooves are cracked & dry & bleeding. i worry the fawn will not survive another walk through the city that the cracks will only get longer & deeper exposing the fawns's legs to grime & trash & infection that can creep up the fawn's legs so that the only thing the fawn can do is lay on a scrap of plastick on a dusty upper level of the old sears building while i listen to the space between each of the fawn's breaths get longer & longer while the stillness of this space grows louder & louder & the moment of transition of this building ends, the building unwrapped from beneath the plastick, unrolled around each tense edge & the new windows carved out from the old stone meet unfiltered light for the first time.

the floors on the upper level are no longer dusty & all the plastick scraps thrown away & the fawn is long gone either held in captivity, shot by animal control or succumbed to infection on that upper level, while i am on the sidewalk looking up @ the whole nation looking down.

# Acknowledgments

FOR ALL THE QUEER/TRANS ARAB PUNKS

NAVIGATING THIS HELLSCAPE

When I left Oakland in May 2018 for New York I wanted to write some kind of love letter to read at my farewell reading. My love for Oakland & my affinities there cannot possibly be contained in a poem or a letter or a moment, so I read from this book, the project that you urged me to complete.

Special thanks to the triad who who saw me in, through & beyond my time in the Bay at that last reading: Andrea Marina, Lara Durback & Juliana Spahr.

This book / I would not exist without my family, friends, lovers & comrades—NM Esc, Binxxx Yglecias, Dorsey Bass, Julia Nakad, Denise Benavides, Alyn Mare, Steffi Zarifis, mai c. doan, Lix Z, Tyler Holmes, Jacky Rossiter, Jasmine Gibson, emji spero, Elizabeth Dake, Davey Davis, Stephanie Young, Joel Gregory, the Intersection of Death crew, & countless others. Thank you for your vast nets of support & uplift. & of course special thanks to my mom, bo & garcie.

Many thanks to the venues where some of these poems originally appeared: *HOLD: A Journal vol.2*, *THE FELT*, & *The Spoon Knife Anthology: Thoughts on Compliance, Defiance, and Resistance*.

Thanks, too, to the many stages, series, basements, rooftops & backyards that encouraged my performances, especially, el Rio, ODC, Counterpulse, Cantil, RADAR, & Woolsey Heights. Bottomless thanks to the STUD for the fabulous cyborg parties & to all the raves, racecars, riots & hot tubs.

Deep gratitude to Kelsey Street Press, Mg Roberts & Jeff Clark who saw this work through to its physical form.

Special thanks to Bhanu Kapil for selecting this assemblage.

In memory of Ara Jo, whose commitment to collective expression, expansiveness & friendship opened up Rock Paper Scissors on monthly Friday nights for Drea & I to host our series, Words of Resistance. Every day, my thoughts are with those lost in the Ghostship fire.

**ANDREA ABI-KARAM** is an arab-american genderqueer punk poet-performer cyborg, writing on the art of killing bros, the intricacies of cyborg bodies, trauma & delayed healing. Their chapbook, *THE AFTERMATH* (Commune Editions, 2016), attempts to queer Fanon's vision of how poetry fails to inspire revolution. Simone White selected Andrea's second assemblage *Villainy* for forthcoming publication with *Les Figues*. They toured with Sister Spit March 2018 & are hype to live in New York. *EXTRATRANSMISSION* is their first book.